What were Shadrach [...] *Abednego called before their names were changed?*

What animal spoke to Balaam when it saw the angel of the Lord?

Whose name always comes last in the Gospels' lists of the twelve apostles?

Who is the only person in scripture who is said to have sneezed?

If you enjoy Bible trivia, you'll love this book! Here are two questions a day for an entire year to test your memory and enhance your knowledge of God's Word.

What can you recall of the people, places, things, and ideas of the Old and New Testaments? *365 Days of Bible Trivia: Questions & Answers for Morning & Evening* will put you to the test.

This is an easy way to impress Bible facts and truths into your memory banks. . .and have fun doing it. Enjoy your year's worth of Bible trivia!

365 DAYS OF
BIBLE
TRIVIA

365 DAYS OF
BIBLE
TRIVIA

QUESTIONS &
ANSWERS
for Morning & Evening

BARBOUR
PUBLISHING

© 2023 by Barbour Publishing, Inc.

ISBN 978-1-63609-498-4

Published by Barbour Publishing, Inc., 1810 Barbour Drive, Uhrichsville, Ohio 44683, www.barbourbooks.com

Our mission is to inspire the world with the life-changing message of the Bible.

ECPA
Evangelical Christian
Publishers Association
Member of the

Printed in China.

Morning

Q: What were Shadrach, Meshach, and Abednego called before their names were changed?

A: Hananiah, Mishael, and Azariah (Daniel 1:7)

Evening

Q: What precious metal covered the ark of the covenant and its carrying poles?

A: Gold (Exodus 25:10-14)

Morning

Q: What did John the Baptist eat?

A: Locusts and wild honey (Matthew 3:4)

Evening

Q: Why did David spare King Saul's life twice?

A: Because Saul was anointed by the Lord (1 Samuel 24:3-6; 26:7-9)

DAY 3

Morning

Q: When Hannah prayed to the Lord for a son, what did she promise?

A: That no razor would touch his head (1 Samuel 1:11)

Evening

Q: What man, with a name like a Roman god, became a powerful preacher of Christ in the early church?

A: Apollos (Acts 18:24-26)

DAY 4

Morning

Q: In the parable of the rich man and Lazarus, where did the poor beggar go when he died?

A: Abraham's bosom (Luke 16:22)

Evening

Q: In addition to Genesis, what other book of the Bible starts, "In the beginning"?

A: John (John 1:1)

DAY 5

Morning

Q: Who discovered baby Moses hidden in the bulrushes of the Nile?

A: Pharaoh's daughter (Exodus 2:3, 5-6)

Evening

Q: Who once carried home two loads of earth from Israel after being healed of leprosy?

A: Naaman (2 Kings 5:13-17)

DAY 6

Morning

Q: Who said, "I see men as trees, walking"?

A: A blind man healed by Jesus (Mark 8:22-25)

Evening

Q: What physical condition of Elisha was once mocked by young people?

A: Baldness (2 Kings 2:23-24)

DAY 7

Morning

Q: What was the covenant that God made with Abraham as he was leaving Haran?

A: "I will make of thee a great nation, and I will bless thee" (Genesis 12:2)

Evening

Q: Who did Pontius Pilate release to the Jews instead of Jesus?

A: Barabbas (Mark 15:15)

DAY 8

Morning

Q: What couple in Acts died after lying about property sold and the money given to the church?

A: Ananias and Sapphira (Acts 5:1–10)

Evening

Q: What were Job's children killed by?

A: Wind (Job 1:19)

DAY 9

Morning

Q: Who built a fleet of trading ships that were wrecked before they ever set sail?

A: King Jehoshaphat (1 Kings 22:48)

Evening

Q: To which church did Paul send these encouraging words: "the Lord is faithful, who shall stablish you, and keep you from evil"?

A: Thessalonica (2 Thessalonians 3:3)

DAY 10

Morning

Q. Where did Peter find a coin to pay the temple tax?

A: In a fish's mouth (Matthew 17:27)

Evening

Q: What was the name of Laban's daughter whom Jacob loved best?

A: Rachel (Genesis 29:16-18)

DAY 11

Morning

Q: What did Moses use to divide the Red Sea?

A: His staff (Exodus 14:16)

Evening

Q: Who brought gifts from the Philippians to Paul while he was imprisoned in Rome?

A: Epaphroditus (Philippians 4:18)

DAY 12

Morning

Q: Who said, "Come, see a man, which told me all things that ever I did"?

A: The Samaritan woman at the well (John 4:7-29)

Evening

Q: Whose sons were consumed by fire for offering an unholy sacrifice in the tabernacle?

A: Aaron's (Leviticus 10:1-2)

DAY 13

Morning

Q: What did Jacob say upon being reunited with Joseph at Goshen?

A: "Now let me die, since I have seen thy face" (Genesis 46:30)

Evening

Q: Who counseled Christians to wait patiently for the Lord, even as a farmer waits "for the precious fruit" and the "early and latter rain"?

A: James (James 5:7)

DAY 14

Morning

Q: What part of Jesus did a sinful woman anoint with perfume and kiss during a dinner at a Pharisee's house?

A: His feet (Luke 7:36-38)

Evening

Q: Who became angry when the people of Nineveh repented after his preaching?

A: Jonah (Jonah 3:2-3, 10; 4:1)

DAY 15

Morning

Q: Why was Miriam stricken with leprosy in the wilderness?

A: She rebelled against Moses' leadership (Numbers 12:1–2, 10)

Evening

Q: What man helped Jesus carry his cross?

A: Simon of Cyrene (Matthew 27:32)

DAY 16

Morning

Q: What three-word question did Pontius Pilate utter after Jesus said He had come into the world "to bear witness unto the truth"?

A: "What is truth?" (John 18:37–38)

Evening

Q: What was the name of Leah's sister?

A: Rachel (Genesis 29:16)

DAY 17

Morning

Q: How long did the Israelites spend in the desert before settling in Canaan?

A: Forty years (Exodus 16:35)

Evening

Q: Which church of Revelation had a reputation for good works but was dead in reality?

A: Sardis (Revelation 3:1)

DAY 18

Morning

Q: What symbolic act did Pontius Pilate perform to try to brush aside responsibility for Jesus' crucifixion?

A: He washed his hands (Matthew 27:24)

Evening

Q: Who became queen by winning a beauty contest?

A: Esther (Esther 2:1-17)

DAY 19

Morning

Q: What was Ebenezer?

A: A stone (1 Samuel 7:12)

Evening

Q: What nickname, meaning "son of consolation [or encouragement]," did the apostles give to Joseph, a Levite from Cyprus?

A: Barnabas (Acts 4:36)

DAY 20

Morning

Q: What did Jesus compare to the movement of God's Spirit?

A: The wind (John 3:8)

Evening

Q: What Canaanite military commander got his head nailed to the ground?

A: Sisera (Judges 4:17, 21)

DAY 21

Morning

Q: What piece of jewelry did Pharaoh give to
Joseph when he made him ruler?

A: A ring (Genesis 41:41–42)

Evening

Q: Which of the ten plagues brought upon Egypt
was darkness?

A: Ninth (Exodus 10:21–29)

DAY 22

Morning

Q: What imprisoned preacher sent his own disciples
to Jesus to ask if He was the expected Messiah?

A: John the Baptist (Matthew 11:1–11)

Evening

Q: What was Adam's occupation while he lived
in Eden?

A: Gardener (Genesis 2:15)

DAY 23

Morning

Q: Whose household was saved in the siege of Jericho by displaying a red cord from a window?

A: Rahab the harlot's (Joshua 2:1, 17-18; 6:16-23)

Evening

Q: What did Jesus say was more likely to go through the eye of a needle than for a rich man to enter heaven?

A: A camel (Matthew 19:24)

DAY 24

Morning

Q: What animal feeding trough served as a temporary bed for the newborn Jesus?

A: A manger (Luke 2:7, 11)

Evening

Q: Who was Solomon's mother?

A: Bathsheba (2 Samuel 12:24)

Morning

Q: What three items were placed in the hands of Gideon's soldiers for the assault on the Midianites?

A: Trumpet, pitcher, and lamp (Judges 7:15-16)

Evening

Q: Who is the world's first murder victim?

A: Abel (Genesis 4:1-8)

Morning

Q: When Jesus said, "Man shall not live by bread alone, but by every word that proceedeth out of the mouth of God," what verse was he quoting?

A: Deuteronomy 0:3 (Matthew 4:4)

Evening

Q: What older cousin adopted the orphaned Esther?

A: Mordecai (Esther 2:7)

DAY 27

Morning

Q: What six-letter word identifies a widespread shortage of food?

A: Famine (Genesis 42:1–5)

Evening

Q: When Isaiah prophesied that a virgin would conceive, whose throne did he say the child would sit on?

A: David's (Isaiah 7:14; 9:7)

DAY 28

Morning

Q: What do we call Jesus' "blessed are they" statements found in the book of Matthew?

A: The Beatitudes (Matthew 5:3–12)

Evening

Q: When Paul was near death in prison, whom did he urge to "come before winter"?

A: Timothy (2 Timothy 1:2; 4:21)

Morning

Q: While Samuel was praying, what did God do to confuse the Philistines who were attacking Israel at Mizpah?

A: He sent thunder (1 Samuel 7:7-10)

Evening

Q: Which of the ten plagues brought upon Egypt turned water to blood?

A: First (Exodus 7:14-25)

Morning

Q: According to James, what has the Lord promised those who endure trials and temptations?

A: The crown of life (James 1:12)

Evening

Q: What prophet was a herdsman from Tekoa?

A: Amos (Amos 1:1)

DAY 31

Morning

Q: What evidence did David produce that he had spared Saul's life in the cave at Engedi?

A: A piece of Saul's robe (1 Samuel 24:1-6)

Evening

Q: On which of the six days of creation did God create light?

A: The first (Genesis 1:3-5)

DAY 32

Morning

Q: Who did Jesus say would award places of honor in the coming kingdom?

A: His Father (Matthew 20:23)

Evening

Q: What mount was frequented by Jesus?

A: Mount of Olives (Luke 22:39)

DAY 33

Morning

Q: What did Moses strike with his staff to get water?

A: The rock of Horeb (Exodus 17:6)

Evening

Q: Who prophesied that the Savior would be born in Bethlehem?

A: Micah (Micah 5:2)

DAY 34

Morning

Q: What two disciples from Jesus' inner circle, described as "unlearned and ignorant men," amazed the Jewish leaders with their courage in preaching the gospel?

A: Peter and John (Acts 4:1-13)

Evening

Q: Why did Naomi and Elimelech leave Bethlehem to settle in Moab?

A: There was famine in Bethlehem (Ruth 1:1-2)

DAY 35

Morning

Q: A prolific writer, Solomon is considered the primary author of which Bible books?

A: Proverbs, Ecclesiastes, and Song of Solomon

Evening

Q: Who anointed Jesus' feet at her home in Bethany?

A: Mary (John 12:1–3)

DAY 36

Morning

Q: In which Bible story did a bird carry an olive leaf?

A: Noah's Ark/the Flood (Genesis 8:1–11)

Evening

Q: In what Bible book do we find these words: "For we are members of his body, of his flesh, and of his bones"?

A: Ephesians (Ephesians 5:30)

DAY 37

Morning

Q: If a cheerful heart is good medicine, what does a crushed spirit do?

A: Dries up the bones (Proverbs 17:22)

Evening

Q: Who went to sleep while Paul was preaching, fell from a window to his death, and was revived by the apostle?

A: Eutychus (Acts 20:9-12)

DAY 38

Morning

Q: In a parable describing the kingdom of heaven, where did Jesus say a man found a hidden treasure?

A: In a field (Matthew 13:44)

Evening

Q: What young prince was hidden in the temple by his aunt for six years to avoid the wrath of Queen Athaliah?

A: Joash (2 Kings 11:2-3)

DAY 39

Morning

Q: What nickname did Jesus give James and John?

A: Sons of Thunder (Mark 3:17)

Evening

Q: Which judge of Israel sacrificed his only child as an offering to God because of a rash promise he made?

A: Jephthah (Judges 11:30–39)

DAY 40

Morning

Q: How did mourners respond when Jesus told them that Jairus' daughter was only sleeping?

A: They laughed at Him (Mark 5:35–40)

Evening

Q: How many days after the resurrection did Jesus ascend into heaven?

A: Forty (Acts 1:3)

Morning

Q: What did Elisha request of Elijah as the prophet was preparing to be taken to heaven in a whirlwind?

A: A "double portion" of Elijah's spirit (2 Kings 2:9–11)

Evening

Q: Besides Jonah, what other prophet ministered in Nineveh?

A: Nahum (Nahum 1:1)

Morning

Q: How did Zacchaeus respond to Jesus' command to come down from the tree?

A: He came down hastily and received Him joyfully (Luke 19:6)

Evening

Q: What new name was given to Jacob after he wrestled with God at the Jabbok River?

A: Israel (Genesis 32:27–28)

DAY 43

Morning

Q: What was Esther's big secret as she competed with other women to become the new queen of Persia?

A: She was Jewish (Esther 2:10; 4:13)

Evening

Q: Who said, "I am the good shepherd: the good shepherd giveth his life for the sheep"?

A: Jesus (John 10:11)

DAY 44

Morning

Q: According to First Thessalonians, whom will God bring with Him when Jesus returns?

A: Those "which sleep in Jesus" (1 Thessalonians 4:14)

Evening

Q: What godly son was born to Hannah and Elkanah in answer to prayer?

A: Samuel (1 Samuel 1:19-20, 27)

DAY 45

Morning

Q: In Jacob's dream, upon what did the angels of God ascend and descend?

A: A ladder (Genesis 28:10-12)

Evening

Q: What animal did Samson use to hold firebrands that destroyed the grain fields of the Philistines?

A: Foxes (Judges 15:4)

DAY 46

Morning

Q: Which of Satan's three temptations of Christ involved a "pinnacle of the temple"?

A: The second (Matthew 4:3-11)

Evening

Q: Who defied her husband to provide food for David's men in the wilderness?

A: Abigail (1 Samuel 25:18-19, 26-27)

DAY 47

Morning

Q: What were the names of Job's three "comforters"?

A: Eliphaz, Bildad, and Zophar (Job 2:11)

Evening

Q: Who said, "Can there any good thing come out of Nazareth?"

A: Nathanael (John 1:46)

DAY 48

Morning

Q: What was Peter doing when the Roman officer's men approached the tanner's house in Joppa?

A: Praying on the housetop (Acts 10:9)

Evening

Q: Whom did the angel of the Lord call "a wild man"?

A: Ishmael (Genesis 16:12)

DAY 49

Morning

Q: Where did God give Moses the Ten Commandments?

A: *Mount Sinai (Exodus 19:20–20:17)*

Evening

Q: Which of the seven deacons of the early church went to Samaria and "preached Christ unto them"?

A: *Philip (Acts 6:5; 8:5)*

DAY 50

Morning

Q: How did Paul answer the question: "Who shall separate us from the love of Christ?"

A: *"Neither death, nor life. . .nor any other creature" (Romans 8:35, 38–39)*

Evening

Q: Who made an ax-head float in the Jordan River?

A: *Elisha (2 Kings 6:1–7)*

Morning

Q: Who killed Jonathan, King Saul's son?

A: The Philistines (1 Chronicles 10:2)

Evening

Q: What king of Israel caused the prophet Samuel to cry to the Lord all night?

A: Saul (1 Samuel 15:11, 26)

Morning

Q: Which two commands did Jesus declare to be the greatest—the substance of all God requires?

A: Love God with all your heart, soul, and mind; and love your neighbor as yourself (Matthew 22:37-40)

Evening

Q: In his message at Pentecost, Peter quoted which prophet to convince the skeptics the disciples were not drunk?

A: Joel (Acts 2:15-17)

Morning

Q: What did God say when Moses doubted His ability to feed the grumbling Hebrews?

A: *"Is the LORD's hand waxed short?"*
(Numbers 11:18–23)

Evening

Q: Who lived longer than anyone else recorded in the Bible?

A: *Methuselah (Genesis 5:27)*

Morning

Q: To what church did Paul give "milk, and not with meat"?

A: *The church at Corinth (1 Corinthians 3:2)*

Evening

Q: Whose staff once budded and produced almonds?

A: *Aaron's (Numbers 17:8)*

DAY 55

Morning

Q: What two prophets encouraged the construction of the second temple in Jerusalem?

A: Haggai and Zechariah (Ezra 5:1-2)

Evening

Q: Who built the first city?

A: Cain (Genesis 4:17)

DAY 56

Morning

Q: What question did a lawyer ask Jesus after He told the man to love God supremely and love his neighbor as himself?

A: "And who is my neighbour?" (Luke 10:29)

Evening

Q: Who said Christ's body was built on the foundation of the apostles and prophets and that Christ was the "chief corner stone"?

A: Paul (Ephesians 2:20)

DAY 57

Morning

Q: What are the four rivers the originated in the garden of Eden?

A: Pison, Gihon, Hiddekel (or Tigris), and Euphrates (Genesis 2:11-14)

Evening

Q: Who put her baby in a basket to save his life?

A: Jochebed (Exodus 2:3; 6:20)

DAY 58

Morning

Q: When Jesus healed the demon-possessed man named Legion, where did the demons go?

A: Into a herd of swine (Luke 8:27-33)

Evening

Q: Who was the prophet Isaiah's father?

A: Amoz (Isaiah 1:1)

DAY 59

Morning

Q: What personal item did Ruth's kinsman present to Boaz as indication he would not redeem Ruth?

A: A shoe or sandal (Ruth 4:5–8)

Evening

Q: Which prophet wrote the shortest book in the Old Testament?

A: Obadiah

DAY 60

Morning

Q: Who is the one authentic mediator between God and man?

A: The man Christ Jesus (1 Timothy 2:5)

Evening

Q: On whose behalf did the apostle Paul write to Philemon?

A: Onesimus (Philemon 10)

DAY 61

Morning

Q: Whose name means "day star"?

A: Lucifer (Isaiah 14:12)

Evening

Q: Who killed a thousand men with a donkey's jawbone?

A: Samson (Judges 15:16)

DAY 62

Morning

Q: In the parable of the good Samaritan, what did the Levite do when he saw a wounded traveler?

A: Looked at him and passed on the other side (Luke 10:30, 32)

Evening

Q: Of the three kings who reigned during the rebuilding of the temple in Jerusalem, who was in power when it was finished?

A: Darius (Ezra 6:15)

DAY 63

Morning

Q: Who lost their garden home, suffered many hardships, and ultimately died because of their sin of disobedience?

A: Adam and Eve (Genesis 3:16-23)

Evening

Q: Who said, "Am I a dog, that thou comest to me with staves [sticks]?"

A: Goliath (1 Samuel 17:43)

DAY 64

Morning

Q: What did Paul tell the Ephesians had broken down the wall separating Jew and Gentile?

A: Christ, by His death on the cross (Ephesians 2:14-16)

Evening

Q: Who said, "Why lodge ye about the wall? if ye do so again, I will lay hands on you"?

A: Nehemiah (Nehemiah 13:21)

Morning

Q: Who said, "How long will it be ere ye make an end of words? mark, and afterwards we will speak"?

A: Bildad, to Job (Job 18:1–2)

Evening

Q: Where was the apostle Paul when he had his hair cut off?

A: Cenchrea (Acts 18:18)

Morning

Q: In Galatians, why did Paul say righteousness could not be attained by "the law"?

A: If so, Christ died in vain (Galatians 2:21)

Evening

Q: What metalworker caused harm to the apostle Paul?

A: Alexander (2 Timothy 4:14)

DAY 67

Morning

Q: What enemy of Israel stole the sacred ark of the covenant and was cursed with many calamities for seven months?

A: The Philistines (1 Samuel 5:11–6:1)

Evening

Q: What businesswoman from Thyatira opened her home to Paul and the saints after her conversion?

A: Lydia (Acts 16:14–15)

DAY 68

Morning

Q: According to the book of Hebrews, how did Christ achieve our eternal redemption without animal sacrifices?

A: By His own shed blood (Hebrews 9:12–14)

Evening

Q: What two men were chosen by God to oversee the making of the ark of the covenant?

A: Bezalel and Aholiab [or Oholiab] (Exodus 31:1–11)

DAY 69

Morning

Q: Who was denied entrance into the promised land for an act of impatience and faithlessness at Meribah?

A: Moses and Aaron (Numbers 20:12-13)

Evening

Q: How many years of famine occurred while Joseph ruled Egypt?

A: Seven (Genesis 41:54)

DAY 70

Morning

Q: What famed evangelist was born to a priest named Zacharias?

A: John the Baptist (Luke 1:57-60)

Evening

Q: What kind of bread were the Israelites to eat in their Passover celebration?

A: Unleavened (Numbers 9:10-11)

DAY 71

Morning

Q: Whom did Elijah defeat on Mount Carmel when fire fell from heaven?

A: Prophets of Baal (1 Kings 18:19, 36–40)

Evening

Q: What judge was nicknamed "Jerubbaal" for tearing down Baal's altar?

A: Gideon (Judges 6:27–32)

DAY 72

Morning

Q: How were the Roman Christians urged to avoid being "conformed to this world"?

A: By the renewing of their minds (Romans 12:2)

Evening

Q: Who said, "O ye dry bones, hear the word of the LORD"?

A: Ezekiel (Ezekiel 37:4)

DAY 73

Morning

Q: Who disobeyed the command of Pharaoh, king of Egypt, to save the male children of the Hebrews?

A: Hebrew midwives, Shiphrah and Puah (Exodus 1:15-17)

Evening

Q: What disciple in Damascus was directed by God to find and assist the newly-converted Saul?

A: Ananias (Acts 9:10-11)

DAY 74

Morning

Q: Upon being released from prison for preaching about Christ, who told authorities: "We ought to obey God rather than men"?

A: Simon Peter (Acts 5:29)

Evening

Q: What was the name of Ruth's sister-in-law?

A: Orpah (Ruth 1:4)

DAY 75

Morning

Q: What two animals appeared in a prophetic vision of Daniel's, near the Ulai River?

A: Ram and goat (Daniel 8:1–12)

Evening

Q: What did the fearful Israelite spies who explored Canaan say they looked like compared to the giants they saw there?

A: Grasshoppers (Numbers 13:33)

DAY 76

Morning

Q: What friend of Jesus braved the early morning darkness alone to visit His tomb?

A: Mary Magdalene (John 20:1)

Evening

Q: What man, for whom a New Testament book is named, traveled to Corinth to help pick up an offering for needy saints?

A: Titus (2 Corinthians 8:16–19)

DAY 77

Morning

Q: What did Solomon request of the Lord as he began his reign?

A: An understanding heart, or wisdom (1 Kings 3:6-9)

Evening

Q: Who was the devout Roman officer instructed in a vision to contact Simon Peter?

A: Cornelius (Acts 10:1-5)

DAY 78

Morning

Q: In Pharaoh's dream, what did the seven lean cows do with the seven fat cows?

A: Ate them (Genesis 41:1-4)

Evening

Q: What disciple, watching Jesus' arrest and trial, claimed three times that he didn't know the Lord?

A: Peter (Matthew 26:69-75)

DAY 79

Morning

Q: What covered the ark of the covenant whenever the Israelite camp moved?

A: The covering veil, or curtain (Numbers 4:5)

Evening

Q: What vegetable did the complaining Israelites recall from their years of slavery in Egypt?

A: Cucumbers (Numbers 11:4-5)

DAY 80

Morning

Q: What did Jesus say He would arrive in when He returns to earth "with power and great glory"?

A: A cloud (Luke 21:27)

Evening

Q: What specific activity did Jesus sometimes forbid to newly-cast out demons?

A: Speaking (Mark 1:34; Luke 4:40-41)

DAY 81

Morning

Q: Why did the Israelites not use leavening in their bread as they left Egypt?

A: There was not time for the dough to rise (Exodus 12:37, 39)

Evening

Q: Who fell off his chair and died when he heard that the ark of the covenant had been stolen?

A: Eli (1 Samuel 4:16-18)

DAY 82

Morning

Q: What did Jesus say the Pharisees would see in response to their demand for a sign from heaven?

A: The sign of Jonah (Matthew 16:1-4)

Evening

Q: How does scripture describe the Moabite king Eglon?

A: "Eglon was a very fat man" (Judges 3:17)

DAY 83

Morning

Q: What kind of knocking accompanied the handwriting on the wall that terrified the Babylonian king Belshazzar?

A: The knocking together of the king's knees (Daniel 5:1–6)

Evening

Q: According to the Proverbs, what do diligent hands bring?

A: Riches or wealth (Proverbs 10:4)

DAY 84

Morning

Q: What did Jesus say a man could forfeit, negating the gain of "the whole world"?

A: His soul (Mark 8:36)

Evening

Q: Which prophet asked if a leopard could change his spots?

A: Jeremiah (Jeremiah 13:23)

Morning

Q: What covenant did God make with Israel as Moses met God on Mount Sinai?

A: "If ye will obey my voice indeed, and keep my covenant, then ye shall be a peculiar treasure unto me above all people" (Exodus 19:1-5)

Evening

Q: Who said, "Weeds were wrapped about my head"?

A: Jonah (Jonah 2:5)

Morning

Q: What "visual aid" did Jesus use to answer the disciples' question, "Who is the greatest in the kingdom of heaven"?

A: A child (Matthew 18:1-4)

Evening

Q: Who kept the ark of the covenant for David and was blessed because of it?

A: Obededom (2 Samuel 6:11)

DAY 87

Morning

Q: What, according to the Song of Songs, cannot quench love?

A: Many waters (Song of Songs 8:7)

Evening

Q: What priestly garment did David use to ask God whether he should pursue the Amalekites, who had kidnapped two of his wives?

A: Ephod (1 Samuel 30:1-8)

DAY 88

Morning

Q: How did Nicodemus defend Jesus when the Jewish leaders were trying to apprehend Him?

A: "Doth our law judge any man, before it hear him?" (John 7:51)

Evening

Q: What troublesome feeling did Paul say is "common to man"?

A: Temptation (1 Corinthians 10:13)

DAY 89

Morning

Q: What does the Bible say turned Solomon's heart from God during the latter years of his life?

A: Foreign wives (1 Kings 11:1-4)

Evening

Q: What substance appeared on Gideon's fleece one night—but not the next—to convince him he was working in God's will?

A: Dew (Judges 6:36-40)

DAY 90

Morning

Q: What did Jesus do for the widow who lived in the town of Nain?

A: Raised her only son from the dead (Luke 7:11-15)

Evening

Q: What son of David cut his long hair whenever it became too heavy for him?

A: Absalom (2 Samuel 14:25-26)

DAY 91

Morning

Q: How was Elijah miraculously fed at the brook Cherith while fleeing from King Ahab?

A: By the ravens (1 Kings 17:1–4)

Evening

Q: What bodily fluid was part of the curse that came by Adam and Eve's sin?

A: Sweat (Genesis 3:19)

DAY 92

Morning

Q: How much did the poor widow whom Jesus commended put in the temple treasury?

A: Two mites, or a farthing (Mark 12:41–42)

Evening

Q: What king unwittingly signed a decree that caused his friend Daniel to be thrown into a den of lions?

A: Darius (Daniel 6:1–16)

Morning

Q: What was Cain's reply when God asked him about his brother?

A: "Am I my brother's keeper?" (Genesis 4:9)

Evening

Q: What tiny seed did Jesus liken the kingdom of heaven to?

A: Mustard (Matthew 13:31–32)

Morning

Q: As Jesus rode into Jerusalem on Palm Sunday, what was His reaction as He looked over the city?

A: He wept over it (Luke 19:28–41)

Evening

Q: Which prophet did King Saul have a medium at Endor call up from the dead?

A: Samuel (1 Samuel 28:1–15)

DAY 95

Morning

Q: What is God's record of all who are saved, as mentioned in Revelation?

A: The Lamb's book of life (Revelation 21:27)

Evening

Q: What "mighty hunter" built Nineveh shortly after Noah's time?

A: Nimrod (Genesis 10:8-11)

DAY 96

Morning

Q: Where did King David take the ark of the covenant where he kept it in a tent?

A: Zion, the City of David (2 Samuel 6:16-17)

Evening

Q: What Jewish ruler was told by Jesus, "Ye must be born again"?

A: Nicodemus (John 3:1-7)

Morning

Q: Whose name always comes last in the Gospels' lists of the twelve apostles?

A: Judas Iscariot (Matthew 10:2-4; Mark 3:16-19)

Evening

Q: What occupation did the apostle Paul have in addition to his missionary duties?

A: Tentmaker (Acts 18:1-3)

Morning

Q: What forbidden tree in the garden of Eden did the serpent convince Eve to eat from?

A: The tree of the knowledge of good and evil (Genesis 2:15 17; 3:1, 6)

Evening

Q: In what New Testament book do we find this title for Christ: "author and finisher of our faith"?

A: Hebrews (Hebrews 12:2)

DAY 99

Morning

Q: What special prisoner was the subject of a letter from Claudius Lysias to Governor Felix?

A: The apostle Paul (Acts 23:25-31)

Evening

Q: What elderly prophetess met Mary, Joseph, and the baby Jesus at the temple and thanked God for the redemption to come?

A: Anna (Luke 2:36-38)

DAY 100

Morning

Q: What three-word title, later applied to Jesus Christ, did the voice of God use to address the prophet Ezekiel?

A: "Son of man" (Ezekiel 2:1; Matthew 8:20)

Evening

Q: What Greek letter did Jesus pair with *Alpha* to describe Himself?

A: Omega (Revelation 22:13)

Morning

Q: What important religious artifact was brought from Zion to the new temple built by Solomon?

A: The ark of the covenant (1 Kings 8:1–5)

Evening

Q: What baking product was banned from Israelite homes for an entire week during the Passover celebration?

A: Leaven, or yeast (Exodus 12:19)

Morning

Q: What tribe did God choose to carry the ark of the covenant?

A: The tribe of Levi (Deuteronomy 10:8)

Evening

Q: What did Jesus do on a Sabbath day that so infuriated the Pharisees they began plotting to kill Him?

A: Heal people (Matthew 12:9–14)

DAY 103

Morning

Q: How did the father of John the Baptist communicate the name of his son to his relatives?

A: He wrote on a tablet (Luke 1:57–63)

Evening

Q: What prophet summoned fire from heaven to destroy fifty-one soldiers carrying King Ahaziah's command to "Come down"?

A: Elijah (2 Kings 1:9–10)

DAY 104

Morning

Q: What did Jesus say God would do for the believers He sees secretly giving to the needy?

A: Reward them (Matthew 6:3–4)

Evening

Q: What fellow government official—formerly an enemy—became Pontius Pilate's friend during Jesus' trial?

A: Herod (Luke 23:5–12)

DAY 105

Morning

Q: What miracle of speech happened to people from many nations gathered at Pentecost?

A: Each heard the gospel in his own language (Acts 2:1–11)

Evening

Q: Whose loss, according to the book of Romans, meant "riches" for the Gentiles?

A: Israel's (Romans 11:7–12)

DAY 106

Morning

Q: Which four men became fairer in countenance through a vegetarian diet?

A: Daniel, Hananiah, Mishael, and Azariah (Daniel 1:11–15)

Evening

Q: What did the psalmist say God's words are sweeter than?

A: Honey (Psalm 119:103)

DAY 107

Morning

Q: What three gifts did the wise men bring to the infant Jesus?

A: Gold, frankincense, and myrrh (Matthew 2:11)

Evening

Q: What kind of bird did God miraculously provide for the Israelites, who had grown tired of manna?

A: Quail (Exodus 16:11-13)

DAY 108

Morning

Q: What portion of Adam's anatomy did God remove to create a companion for the man?

A: A rib (Genesis 2:22)

Evening

Q: What captain in Deborah's army is listed in Hebrews as a hero of faith?

A: Barak (Judges 4:14-15; Hebrews 11:32-34)

DAY 109

Morning

Q: Where was the young Jesus found after He was missing for three days following the Feast of the Passover?

A: In the temple with the teachers (Luke 2:41-46)

Evening

Q: What king of Israel was known for his furious chariot driving?

A: Jehu (2 Kings 9:20)

DAY 110

Morning

Q: Which four little creatures are said to be exceedingly wise?

A: Ants, conies, locusts, and spiders (or lizards) (Proverbs 30:24-28)

Evening

Q: What position of authority did Pontius Pilate hold?

A: Governor (Matthew 27:2)

DAY 111

Morning

Q: What did the persecutor Saul do when a light from heaven flashed around him?

A: He fell to the ground (Acts 9:3–4)

Evening

Q: What daughter of Bethuel was wife of the patriarch Isaac?

A: Rebekah (Genesis 25:20)

DAY 112

Morning

Q: How did Ruth show her interest in Boaz at the threshing floor?

A: She lay at his feet (Ruth 3:2–5)

Evening

Q: What man, described in Acts as "full of faith and of the Holy Ghost," was one of seven chosen to relieve the apostles of waiting on tables?

A: Stephen (Acts 6:1–5)

DAY 113

Morning

Q: What group of people will be called "the children of God"?

A: The peacemakers (Matthew 5:9)

Evening

Q: What rivers did Naaman, the leprous Syrian army commander, prefer to wash in to cleanse his disease?

A: Abana and Pharpar (2 Kings 5:10–14)

DAY 114

Morning

Q: What were the Ten Commandments engraved on?

A: Two tablets of stone (Deuteronomy 4:13)

Evening

Q: What great-grandson of Ruth became a king of Israel?

A: David (Ruth 4:13–17)

Morning

Q: How did Jesus spend the night before choosing His apostles?

A: He prayed all night on a mountain (Luke 6:12-13)

Evening

Q: What devout man held the baby Jesus when Mary and Joseph presented Him at the temple?

A: Simeon (Luke 2:25-32)

Morning

Q: How did Joseph answer his fearful brothers who expected retaliation after their father's death?

A: "Fear not: for am I in the place of God?" (Genesis 50:15, 19-20)

Evening

Q: What king of Assyria insulted God to King Hezekiah of Judah—and paid for it with his life?

A: Sennacherib (2 Kings 19:5-13, 35-37)

Morning

Q: What did Jesus say to Jairus, the synagogue ruler, when Jesus was told the ruler's daughter had died?

A: "Be not afraid, only believe" (Mark 5:35-36)

Evening

Q: What man, a Horonite, opposed Nehemiah and the Jews rebuilding the walls of Jerusalem?

A: Sanballat (Nehemiah 2:10; 4:1-2)

Morning

Q: Who held up Moses' hands at Rephidim while Joshua battled the Amalekites?

A: Aaron and Hur (Exodus 17:12-13)

Evening

Q: How many days had Jesus fasted in the desert when Satan tempted Him to turn stones into bread?

A: Forty (Matthew 4:1-4)

Morning

Q: What will happen to believers who are alive when Jesus appears in the clouds?

A: They will be caught up to meet the Lord in the air (1 Thessalonians 4:16-17)

Evening

Q: What mount saw the deaths of King Saul and his sons in battle?

A: Gilboa (1 Samuel 31:8)

Morning

Q: What structure in Jerusalem did Zechariah, son of Jonathan, help Nehemiah dedicate?

A: The wall (Nehemiah 12:27-37)

Evening

Q: What type of tree immediately withered when Jesus cursed it—an event Jesus used to teach His disciples about faith?

A: Fig (Matthew 21:18-22)

DAY 121

Morning

Q: After Saul was converted and baptized, where did he go to witness for Christ?

A: To the synagogues (Acts 9:18-20)

Evening

Q: What city was the hometown of the apostle Paul?

A: Tarsus (Acts 22:2-3)

DAY 122

Morning

Q: Who is the only person in scripture who is said to have sneezed?

A: The Shunammite woman's son (2 Kings 4:25-35)

Evening

Q: What man, attempting to steady the ark of the covenant on its cart, was struck dead for touching it?

A: Uzzah (2 Samuel 6:6-7)

DAY 123

Morning

Q: What unnamed woman from Samaria did Jesus offer the "living water" to?

A: The woman at the well (John 4:7, 10)

Evening

Q: In which Bible book is a rainbow first mentioned?

A: Genesis (Genesis 9:13)

DAY 124

Morning

Q: What grew from the ground God cursed after Adam and Eve's sin?

A: Thorns and thistles (Genesis 3:17–18)

Evening

Q: In what city did silversmiths—fearing the effect of Paul's preaching on their idol-making business—stir up a riot?

A: Ephesus (Acts 19:25–32)

Morning

Q: In Jesus' parable of the sower, what does the seed represent?

A: God's word or message (Mark 4:14)

Evening

Q: How many leprous men came to Jesus requesting a mass healing—for which only one returned to praise God?

A: Ten (Luke 17:11–19)

Morning

Q: What did God give Saul after he was anointed king?

A: "Another heart," or a new nature (1 Samuel 10:9)

Evening

Q: What suffering Old Testament saint complained that God would "terrify" him with visions?

A: Job (Job 7:13–14)

DAY 127

Morning

Q: What did Paul tell Timothy about those who do not provide for their own households?

A: *They have denied the faith and are worse than infidels (1 Timothy 5:8)*

Evening

Q: What apostle had a vision of animals being let down from heaven in a sheet—and realized God had offered salvation to the Gentiles?

A: *Peter (Acts 11:4-18)*

DAY 128

Morning

Q: What did the psalmist say would follow him all the days of his life?

A: *Goodness and mercy (Psalm 23:6)*

Evening

Q: What precious substance, according to Proverbs, cannot compare to the value of wisdom?

A: *Gold (Proverbs 16:16)*

DAY 129

Morning

Q: Who did Jesus liken to a man who built his house upon a rock?

A: One who hears and obeys Christ's sayings (Matthew 7:24)

Evening

Q: What second wife of Elkanah provoked his other wife, Hannah, over her barrenness?

A: Peninnah (1 Samuel 1:1-6)

DAY 130

Morning

Q: Where did the Levite priests store the Ten Commandments in the temple?

A: In the ark of the covenant (Deuteronomy 31:9, 26)

Evening

Q: What did the apostle Paul, writing to the Thessalonians, say that those who refused to work should be kept from doing?

A: Eating (2 Thessalonians 3:10)

DAY 131

Morning

Q: In describing a guest of honor and a servant at a banquet, who did Jesus identify with?

A: The servant (Luke 22:27)

Evening

Q: What word did the writer of Ecclesiastes use to describe the sleep of a laborer?

A: Sweet (Ecclesiastes 5:12)

DAY 132

Morning

Q: What was Saul looking for when he met Samuel for the first time?

A: Lost donkeys (1 Samuel 9:3, 6, 14)

Evening

Q: What Old Testament woman was buried in a cave in the field of Machpelah?

A: Sarah (Genesis 23:19)

DAY 133

Morning

Q: How did Nicodemus react to Jesus' statement that a man must have a second birth?

A: "How can a man be born when he is old?" (John 3:1-4)

Evening

Q: What melting substance did the psalmist say his heart had turned to?

A: Wax (Psalm 22:14)

DAY 134

Morning

Q: What idol were the Israelites worshipping with shouting and singing when Moses arrived with God's Ten Commandments?

A: The golden calf (Exodus 32:1-4, 17-20)

Evening

Q: What nationality, hated by Jews, provided the "good guy" character in Jesus' parable of a man beaten by robbers?

A: Samaritan (Luke 10:25-37)

DAY 135

Morning

Q: What happened to the sky between the sixth and ninth hours as Jesus approached death?

A: Darkness came over the land (Matthew 27:45-50)

Evening

Q: What modern-day nation, with its capital at New Delhi, marked the eastern extent of King Ahasuerus' nation?

A: India (Esther 8:9)

DAY 136

Morning

Q: In crossing the Jordan at Jericho, what was the significance of the twelve memorial stones taken from the river?

A: That Israel crossed the Jordan on dry ground (Joshua 4:20-23)

Evening

Q: Which early Christian martyr died with the consent of Saul of Tarsus?

A: Stephen (Acts 7:58-59; 8:1)

Morning

Q: How did the centurion Cornelius receive Peter when they met at Caesarea?

A: He fell at his feet before him (Acts 10:24-25)

Evening

Q: What great prophet heard God say, "Man looketh on the outward appearance, but the LORD looketh on the heart"?

A: Samuel (1 Samuel 16:7)

Morning

Q: How did Ahab greet the prophet Elijah when he called on the king during an extended drought?

A: "Art thou he that troubleth Israel?"
(1 Kings 18:16-17)

Evening

Q: What wayward prophet was thrown overboard by pagan sailors frightened by a violent storm at sea?

A: Jonah (Jonah 1:13-15)

DAY 139

Morning

Q: Why was the woman at the well surprised when Jesus spoke to her?

A: He was a Jew; she was a Samaritan (John 4:9)

Evening

Q: What son of David tried to usurp the throne and was ultimately executed by Solomon?

A: Adonijah (1 Kings 1–2)

DAY 140

Morning

Q: What animal spoke to Balaam when it saw the angel of the Lord?

A: An ass, or donkey (Numbers 22:27–28)

Evening

Q: What was Jesus doing in a boat immediately before calming a storm that terrified His disciples?

A: Sleeping (Luke 8:22–25)

Morning

Q: How much money was Judas promised for betraying Jesus?

A: *Thirty pieces of silver (Matthew 26:14-15)*

Evening

Q: What conspiring son of King David caused his father to flee for his life from Jerusalem?

A: *Absalom (2 Samuel 15:13-37)*

Morning

Q: How did young Samson demonstrate his strength while going through the vineyard at Timnath?

A: *By killing a lion barehanded (Judges 14:5-6)*

Evening

Q: On which of the six days of creation did God create the animals?

A: *Sixth (Genesis 1:24-31)*

DAY 143

Morning

Q: Why did Philip leave his great work in Samaria to travel the road from Jerusalem to Gaza?

A: He was directed by an angel to do so (Acts 8:25–26)

Evening

Q: What Old Testament prophet, who called himself "a child," wore a wooden yoke as an object lesson?

A: Jeremiah (Jeremiah 1:6; 27:1–2; 28:12–14)

DAY 144

Morning

Q: What weapon did the young David use to slay the giant warrior Goliath?

A: A sling (1 Samuel 17:4, 50)

Evening

Q: How old was the boy Jesus when He amazed people in the temple with His spiritual insights?

A: Twelve (Luke 2:41–52)

Morning

Q: What words did Jesus use when He committed His mother, Mary, to John's care?

A: "Behold thy mother!" (John 19:25-27)

Evening

Q: What instrument did the young David play to soothe the troubled spirit of King Saul?

A: Harp (1 Samuel 16:23)

Morning

Q: Who were the three sons of Noah?

A: Shem, Ham, and Japheth (Genesis 6:10)

Evening

Q: What famous tree of Lebanon was used by the psalmist as a metaphor for the righteous?

A: Cedar (Psalm 92:12)

DAY 147

Morning

Q: What did Peter do after his third denial of
Christ and the crowing of the rooster?

A: He wept bitterly (Luke 22:54-62)

Evening

Q: What Egyptian crops were destroyed by the
plague of hail called down by Moses?

A: Flax and barley (Exodus 9:29-31)

DAY 148

Morning

Q: Whom did Elijah revive from the dead at the
home of the widow in Zarephath?

A: Her son (1 Kings 17:9, 20-22)

Evening

Q: What city was the site of King Ahasuerus' royal
citadel?

A: Shushan, or Susa (Esther 1:2)

Morning

Q: How many people believed, were baptized, and joined the church after Peter's message on Pentecost?

A: About three thousand (Acts 2:38-41)

Evening

Q: What physical characteristic initially hindered Zacchaeus from seeing Jesus?

A: Shortness (Luke 19:2-3)

Morning

Q: What miracle occurred in the heavens the day Joshua and the Israelites defeated the armies of the five kings of the Amorites?

A: The sun stood still (Joshua 10:12-14)

Evening

Q: What Philistine city's name is still heard in the news today, sometimes with the word "strip"?

A: Gaza (2 Kings 18:8)

Morning

Q: Why did James indicate that we do not always receive from God?

A: We do not ask (James 4:2)

Evening

Q: What town, along with Bethsaida, did not repent when Jesus performed miracles there and thus received a pronouncement of woe?

A: Chorazin, or Korazin (Matthew 11:20-21)

Morning

Q: What sign did God give David as a signal to attack the Philistines at Rephaim Valley?

A: The sound of marching in the treetops (2 Samuel 5:17-25)

Evening

Q: What annual celebration was instituted to commemorate the Jews' victory over their enemies in Queen Esther's time?

A: Purim (Esther 9:20-28)

Morning

Q: What idol kept falling on its face in front of the ark of the covenant?

A: Dagon (1 Samuel 5:3)

Evening

Q: What "prince of the devils" did Pharisees accuse Jesus of using to cast out demons?

A: Beelzebub (Mark 3:22)

Morning

Q: What two foods were said to flow in the land of Canaan?

A: Milk and honey (Numbers 13:27)

Evening

Q: What type of tree surrounded a man on a red horse in a vision of the prophet Zechariah?

A: Myrtle (Zechariah 1:7-8)

Morning

Q: What constrained Paul to appeal to the Romans to present themselves as a "living sacrifice. . . unto God"?

A: The mercies of God (Romans 12:1)

Evening

Q: What king of Israel captured the fortress of Zion from mocking Jebusites?

A: David (2 Samuel 5:6-8)

Morning

Q: Whose tomb was marked by a pillar erected by her husband, Jacob?

A: Rachel (Genesis 35:19-20)

Evening

Q: What were Peter, James, and John doing while Jesus was praying and agonizing in Gethsemane?

A: Sleeping (Matthew 26:36-40)

Morning

Q: In Peter's sermon on the day of Pentecost, what did he offer those who repented and were baptized in Christ's name?

A: The gift of the Holy Spirit (Acts 2:1, 14, 38)

Evening

Q: What was the name of Ruth's first husband, who died?

A: Mahlon (Ruth 4:10)

Morning

Q: What were the Bereans famous for?

A: Searching the scriptures (Acts 17:11)

Evening

Q: Who said, "O LORD, take, I beseech thee, my life from me; for it is better for me to die than to live"?

A: Jonah (Jonah 4:3)

Morning

Q: How did the Jewish leaders know where to find Jesus in the garden of Gethsemane?

A: Judas led them to Him (John 18:2-3, 5)

Evening

Q: What relative do the Proverbs say a young man should call "wisdom"?

A: Sister (Proverbs 7:4)

Morning

Q: Where did Abraham almost sacrifice his son Isaac?

A: Moriah, which Abraham called Jehovah-Jireh (Genesis 22:1-14)

Evening

Q: What king, the son of Solomon, threatened to place his subjects under a heavy yoke—and caused many of the tribes of Israel to rebel?

A: Rehoboam (1 Kings 12:1-19)

Morning

Q: Where did Peter go to join other believers when he was delivered from Herod's prison?

A: The house of Mary, mother of John Mark (Acts 12:7-12)

Evening

Q: How many of those "redeemed from the earth" stood with the Lamb on Mount Zion in John's Revelation?

A: 144,000 (Revelation 14:1-3)

Morning

Q: With what words did Isaiah accept God's call to service the year King Uzziah died?

A: "Here am I; send me" (Isaiah 6:1, 8)

Evening

Q: What was the first name of the apostle known as "Zelotes" or "the Zealot"?

A: Simon (Luke 6:12-16)

DAY 163

Morning

Q: What title was used by the voice from heaven to describe Jesus following His baptism?

A: "My beloved Son" (Matthew 3:16-17)

Evening

Q: Which king installed waterworks in Jerusalem?

A: Hezekiah (2 Kings 20:20)

DAY 164

Morning

Q: What was Moses doing when God spoke to him in the burning bush?

A: Herding sheep (Exodus 3:1-4)

Evening

Q: In what Roman province were the seven churches of Revelation located?

A: Asia (Revelation 1:11)

DAY 165

Morning

Q: What did Paul tell the Corinthians that the believer's temporary "light affliction" would result in?

A: Much greater eternal glory (2 Corinthians 4:17)

Evening

Q: Whom did Paul instruct to counsel the "rich in this world" to trust in the living God rather than their "uncertain riches"?

A: Timothy (1 Timothy 6:17)

DAY 166

Morning

Q: How did God quench Samson's thirst after the victory at Lehi?

A: A spring opened up (Judges 15:12-19)

Evening

Q: What synagogue official saw his twelve-year-old daughter raised to life by Jesus?

A: Jairus (Luke 8:41-56)

DAY 167

Morning

Q: In Jesus' parable of the ten virgins, why were five foolish women not prepared to enter the bridal party?

A: They had no oil in their lamps (Matthew 25:1–8)

Evening

Q: What type of tree does the love-smitten woman of the Song of Songs compare her man to?

A: Apple (Song of Songs 2:3)

DAY 168

Morning

Q: What did Hannah make for Samuel each year of his childhood?

A: A coat (1 Samuel 1:20; 2:19)

Evening

Q: What kind of stone, according to the apostle Paul, did God lay in Zion?

A: Stumbling (Romans 9:32–33)

Morning

Q: According to Paul's message in Athens, what assurance has God given us that Christ will judge the world?

A: God raised Jesus from the dead (Acts 17:16, 31)

Evening

Q: What king of Israel solved a child custody dispute by proposing that the child be cut in half?

A: Solomon (1 Kings 3:15, 25-27)

Morning

Q: After Noah left the ark, what was his first recorded action?

A: He built an altar to the Lord (Genesis 8:18-20)

Evening

Q: Which king failed to give glory to God and was struck dead by an angel and eaten by worms?

A: Herod (Acts 12:21-23)

DAY 171

Morning

Q: In Ephesians, why did Paul tell us salvation could not be accomplished by "works"?

A: Lest men should boast (Ephesians 2:8-9)

Evening

Q: Who ministered to Jesus after Satan finished his temptations?

A: Angels (Matthew 4:11)

DAY 172

Morning

Q: What was the answer to Samson's riddle, "Out of the eater came forth meat, and out of the strong came forth sweetness"?

A: Honey from a lion's carcass (Judges 14:12-18)

Evening

Q: Who wrote that the purpose of the law was to give knowledge of sin and establish guilt?

A: Paul (Romans 3:19-20)

DAY 173

Morning

Q: What did Jesus promise two fishermen if they would follow Him?

A: He'd make them "fishers of men"
(Matthew 4:18-19)

Evening

Q: Who was the surviving member of King Saul's family to whom David showed kindness?

A: Mephibosheth (2 Samuel 9:6-7)

DAY 174

Morning

Q: What motivated a crowd at Lystra to proclaim Paul and Barnabas as gods?

A: The healing of a crippled man (Acts 14:8-12)

Evening

Q: What sorcerer at Paphos was struck blind by Paul for his heresy?

A: Barjesus, or Elymas (Acts 13:6, 8-11)

DAY 175

Morning

Q: According to Paul, what ministry has God assigned to Christians since God "hath reconciled us to himself by Jesus Christ"?

A: The ministry of reconciliation (2 Corinthians 5:18)

Evening

Q: How does the Bible describe the serpent that tempted Eve to sin against God?

A: "Subtil," or crafty (Genesis 3:1)

DAY 176

Morning

Q: In God's perfect kingdom, the wolf will dwell with what?

A: The lamb (Isaiah 11:6)

Evening

Q: Who grieved at the death of her brother and appealed to Jesus for help?

A: Martha (John 11:18–22)

Morning

Q: What did a voice from heaven instruct Peter to do when he fell into a trance?

A: "Rise, Peter; kill, and eat" (Acts 10:9–13)

Evening

Q: The second temple, completed by returned exiles, is known by what name?

A: Zerubbabel's (Zechariah 4:9)

Morning

Q: How did God evaluate His work after six days of creative labor?

A: All He made was "very good" (Genesis 1:31)

Evening

Q: What respected Pharisee told the Jewish council that if the apostles' witness "be of God, ye cannot overthrow it"?

A: Gamaliel (Acts 5:34, 38–39)

DAY 179

Morning

Q: What charge was made by false witnesses against Jesus before Caiaphas, the high priest?

A: That Jesus said He could destroy the temple and rebuild it in three days (Matthew 26:57-61)

Evening

Q: What was Jesus' destination when He left Judea and passed through Samaria?

A: Galilee (John 4:3-4)

DAY 180

Morning

Q: How did the believers react to Saul when he returned to Jerusalem after his conversion?

A: They were afraid of him (Acts 9:22, 26)

Evening

Q: In what Old Testament book do we find this promise: "Cast thy bread upon the waters: for thou shalt find it after many days"?

A: Ecclesiastes (Ecclesiastes 11:1)

Morning

Q: How did Nicodemus express devotion to Jesus after He was crucified?

A: He brought spices to anoint Christ's body
(John 19:39–40)

Evening

Q: What did Paul say was the last enemy of believers to be destroyed?

A: Death (1 Corinthians 15:26)

Morning

Q: What fruit "of the eye" is mentioned several times in the Old Testament?

A: Apple (Deuteronomy 32:10; Psalm 17:8;
Proverbs 7:2; Lamentations 2:18; Zechariah 2:8)

Evening

Q: Who was swallowed up by the earth, along with his fellow conspirators, in a rebellion against Moses and Aaron?

A: Korah (Numbers 16:1–2, 32–33)

DAY 183

Morning

Q: What were Jesus' final words before His death?

A: "Father, into thy hands I commend my spirit" (Luke 23:46)

Evening

Q: What servant girl met Peter at the believers' door after an angel had freed him from prison?

A: Rhoda (Acts 12:13)

DAY 184

Morning

Q: What did David win by defeating Goliath?

A: A wife (1 Samuel 17:25-26; 18:17-22)

Evening

Q: Who was Jacob's only daughter?

A: Dinah (Genesis 34:1)

DAY 185

Morning

Q: What phrase did Jesus use to describe Himself after feeding the five thousand men?

A: "Bread of life" (John 6:10, 35)

Evening

Q: Who introduced Simon Peter to Jesus?

A: Peter's brother Andrew (John 1:40-42)

DAY 186

Morning

Q: In Joseph's dream, what did the sun and moon stand for?

A: His parents (Genesis 37:5, 9-10)

Evening

Q: According to the Proverbs, all hard work brings profit—but what does all talk bring?

A: Penury, or poverty (Proverbs 14:23)

DAY 187

Morning

Q: What is the meaning of "Corban," a practice adopted by some Jews to avoid caring for their parents?

A: A gift dedicated to God (Mark 7:11–13)

Evening

Q: What son of Jared lived "only" 365 years but didn't die—because God took him away?

A: Enoch (Genesis 5:18, 23–24; Hebrews 11:5)

DAY 188

Morning

Q: In what room of the first temple was the ark of the covenant kept?

A: The most holy place (1 Kings 8:6)

Evening

Q: To which church did the apostle Paul say he rejoiced "in my sufferings for you, and fill up that which is behind of the afflictions of Christ in my flesh for his body's sake, which is the church"?

A: Colosse (Colossians 1:24)

DAY 189

Morning

Q: According to Ephesians, what part of Christians' armor equips them to "quench all the fiery darts of the wicked"?

A: The shield of faith (Ephesians 6:16)

Evening

Q: Who went around stripped and barefoot for three years as a sign against Egypt?

A: Isaiah (Isaiah 20:3)

DAY 190

Morning

Q: What did Jeremiah, Daniel, and Isaiah have in common?

A: They were prophets

Evening

Q: What prophet was taken alive to heaven in a whirlwind?

A: Elijah (2 Kings 2:11)

Morning

Q: In Philippians, what reason does Paul give for Christ's exaltation by the Father?

A: He humbled Himself and became obedient unto death (Philippians 2:8–11)

Evening

Q: Who stole treasure from the devastated city of Jericho—and paid for his sin with his life?

A: Achan (Joshua 7)

Morning

Q: What did Paul tell Timothy was the root of all evil?

A: "The love of money" (1 Timothy 6:10)

Evening

Q: Who wrote that church members are living stones composing a spiritual house that offers up "spiritual sacrifices, acceptable to God"?

A: Peter (1 Peter 2:5)

DAY 193

Morning

Q: What did James advise those lacking wisdom
to do?

A: Ask of God (James 1:5)

Evening

Q: To whom did Paul address these words: "Endure
hardness, as a good soldier of Jesus Christ"?

A: Timothy (2 Timothy 2:3)

DAY 194

Morning

Q: When Jesus died on the cross, what was torn
in two?

A: The veil in the temple (Matthew 27:50-51)

Evening

Q: Which of Joseph's brothers urged that his life be
spared?

A: Reuben (Genesis 37:21)

Morning

Q: Who was turned into a pillar of salt for looking back at the destruction of a wicked city?

A: Lot's wife (Genesis 19:23-26)

Evening

Q: What wife of King Herod engineered the execution of John the Baptist?

A: Herodias (Mark 6:14-29)

Morning

Q: Why did people of Jesus' day go to the pool of Bethesda?

A: To be healed (John 5:1-4)

Evening

Q: Who instructed believers to "try the spirits whether they are of God" or the "spirit of antichrist"?

A: John (1 John 4:1-3)

Morning

Q: According to Ephesians, how did Christ abolish the wall dividing Jew and Gentile and establish peace?

A: By the death of His physical body (Ephesians 2:14-15)

Evening

Q: To which church did Paul address these words: "Grieve not the holy Spirit of God, whereby ye are sealed unto the day of redemption"?

A: Ephesus (Ephesians 4:30)

Morning

Q: In the parable of the Good Samaritan, what condition was the traveler in when the thieves left him?

A: Almost naked and half dead (Luke 10:30)

Evening

Q: What wealthy but foolish man from Carmel refused food to David's men and was smitten by the Lord?

A: Nabal (1 Samuel 25:9-12, 37-38)

DAY 199

Morning

Q: What did Paul promise the Galatians who did not become "weary in well doing"?

A: *They would reap in due time if they didn't faint (Galatians 6:9)*

Evening

Q: What was the supposed fertility root mentioned in the story of Jacob, Leah, and Rachel?

A: *Mandrake (Genesis 30:14)*

DAY 200

Morning

Q: What was the first question of God's recorded in the Bible?

A: *His question to Adam, "Where art thou?" (Genesis 3:9)*

Evening

Q: What town was home to Zacchaeus?

A: *Jericho (Luke 19:1, 5-6)*

Morning

Q: To what did James liken a tongue out of control?

A: Fire from hell (James 3:6)

Evening

Q: In what city of Samaria did Jesus meet the woman at Jacob's well?

A: Sychar (John 4:5-7)

Morning

Q: Whom will Christ send to gather the redeemed when He returns to earth?

A: His angels (Matthew 24:30-31)

Evening

Q: On which of the six days of creation did God create the sun, moon, and stars?

A: Fourth (Genesis 1:14-19)

DAY 203

Morning

Q: What Christian virtue does John say is the victory that overcomes the world?

A: Our faith (1 John 5:4)

Evening

Q: What did the apostle Paul write is the "fulfilling of the law"?

A: Love (Romans 13:8, 10)

DAY 204

Morning

Q: What was Adam's punishment for disobeying God in the garden of Eden?

A: Banishment, and the need to till the ground (Genesis 3:21–24)

Evening

Q: Where did Paul tell the Philippians the Christian's ultimate citizenship is located?

A: Heaven (Philippians 3:20)

Morning

Q: What is another name the for Lake of Gennesaret?

A: The Sea of Galilee (Luke 5:1)

Evening

Q: What judge of Israel had thirty sons who rode thirty donkeys?

A: Jair (Judges 10:3)

Morning

Q: What name did Jesus give Peter that was prophetic of his maturity as a Christian leader?

A: Cephas, meaning "a stone" or "rock" (John 1:42)

Evening

Q: What kind of serpent did Moses lift up on a pole to save the Israelites from a plague of venomous snakes?

A: Brass (Numbers 21:9)

Morning

Q: Which two churches of Revelation were chastised for tolerating false teachers?

A: Pergamos and Thyatira
(Revelation 2:12-15, 18-20)

Evening

Q: Who interceded for Paul when the believers at Jerusalem were reluctant to accept him as a convert?

A: Barnabas (Acts 9:26-28)

Morning

Q: What collapsed and killed eighteen people in a "news event" that Jesus used to encourage repentance?

A: A tower (Luke 13:2-5)

Evening

Q: Where were the Hebrew captives when Jeremiah advised them to "seek the peace of the city"?

A: Babylon (Jeremiah 29:1, 7)

DAY 209

Morning

Q: How did the woman with an issue of blood express her faith in Jesus?

A: She touched His clothes (Mark 5:25-29)

Evening

Q: What church was challenged to speak the truth in love and grow up to be Christlike in all things?

A: Ephesus (Ephesians 4:15)

DAY 210

Morning

Q: Where did Christ say the "gospel of the kingdom" would be preached before the end of time arrived?

A: "In all the world" (Matthew 24:14)

Evening

Q: Who saw a vision of a sheet lowered from heaven with living creatures on it?

A: Peter (Acts 10:9-12)

DAY 211

Morning

Q: According to Ephesians, where did the Father seat Christ after raising Him from the dead?

A: At His right hand in heaven (Ephesians 1:20, 22)

Evening

Q: What companion chronicled much of Paul's missionary activities in Acts?

A: Luke (Acts 1:1; 16:10; Luke 1:3)

DAY 212

Morning

Q: How old was Adam when he died?

A: 930 years old (Genesis 5:5)

Evening

Q: Who wrote these words to believers in Asia Minor: "Honour all men. Love the brotherhood. . . . Honour the king"?

A: Peter (1 Peter 2:17)

DAY 213

Morning

Q: What did Zacchaeus volunteer to do for the poor after his encounter with Jesus?

A: Give them half his wealth (Luke 19:8)

Evening

Q: What Old Testament prophet did God assign as a "watchman unto the house of Israel" to warn them of coming judgment?

A: Ezekiel (Ezekiel 33:7-8)

DAY 214

Morning

Q: What was Jesus holding when He asked whose picture was on it?

A: A coin (Matthew 22:19-21)

Evening

Q: To whom did God say: "In the sweat of thy face shalt thou eat bread"?

A: Adam (Genesis 3:17-19)

DAY 215

Morning

Q: How did Jesus describe Himself to Martha prior to raising Lazarus from the dead?

A: "The resurrection, and the life" (John 11:25, 43–44)

Evening

Q: How many braids did Samson have in his hair?

A: Seven (Judges 16:19)

DAY 216

Morning

Q: What significant event concerning man's lifespan occurred during Noah's time?

A: It was shortened to 120 years (Genesis 5:32–6:3)

Evening

Q: Which angel told Mary that she would have the baby Jesus?

A: Gabriel (Luke 1:26–31)

DAY 217

Morning

Q: What did Jesus say are like wolves?

A: False prophets (Matthew 7:15)

Evening

Q: Who wrote the most Bible books?

A: Paul—with at least thirteen

DAY 218

Morning

Q: What did God make man a little lower than?

A: The angels (Psalm 8:4-5)

Evening

Q: What Persian queen refused to display her beauty at the court of King Ahasuerus?

A: Vashti (Esther 1:11-12)

Morning

Q: Who told Jesus about a problem, which He solved by doing His first recorded miracle?

A: Mary, His mother (John 2:1-11)

Evening

Q: Whom did Paul commend for a genuine faith that also characterized his mother and grandmother?

A: Timothy (2 Timothy 1:5)

Morning

Q: What did Paul write to the Corinthians that "we are not ignorant of" regarding Satan?

A: His devices, or schemes (2 Corinthians 2:11)

Evening

Q: How many disciples did Jesus send to get a donkey for His ride to Jerusalem?

A: Two (Matthew 21:1-3)

DAY 221

Morning

Q: What blind beggar in Jericho received his sight from Jesus?

A: Bartimaeus (Mark 10:46-52)

Evening

Q: Where did Jonah try to go to avoid his responsibilities in Nineveh?

A: Tarshish (Jonah 1:3)

DAY 222

Morning

Q: Why was the lame man Jesus healed by the sheep market pool criticized by the Jews?

A: He was carrying his bed on the Sabbath (John 5:1, 8-10)

Evening

Q: Who asked God, "What is man, that thou art mindful of him?"

A: David (Psalm 8:4)

DAY 223

Morning

Q: What two books in the Bible are named after women?

A: Esther and Ruth

Evening

Q: To which apostle did Jesus speak the words, "I am the way, the truth, and the life: no man cometh unto the Father, but by me"?

A: Thomas (John 14:5-6)

DAY 224

Morning

Q: How did the crowd react to Jesus' friendship with Zacchaeus?

A: They murmured that Jesus was dining with a sinner (Luke 19:5-7)

Evening

Q: For how many days did the Egyptians mourn the death of Jacob?

A: Seventy (Genesis 50:1-3)

Morning

Q: What was Matthew's vocation before he became a disciple of Jesus?

A: Publican, or tax collector
(Matthew 9:9; Luke 5:27)

Evening

Q: According to Revelation, what is "the number of the beast"?

A: Six hundred threescore and six, or 666
(Revelation 13:18)

Morning

Q: After the Ethiopian eunuch accepted Jesus, what did he request of Philip?

A: To be baptized (Acts 8:35–37)

Evening

Q: Which New Testament book contains the words, "Without faith it is impossible to please him"?

A: Hebrews (Hebrews 11:6)

Morning

Q: Who is the "father of lies"?

A: The devil (John 8:44)

Evening

Q: Which Bible character said, "To whom would the king delight to do honour more than to myself?"

A: Haman (Esther 6:6)

Morning

Q: Who wore clothing made of camel's hair?

A: John the Baptist (Matthew 3:1–4)

Evening

Q: Who penned the words, "It is better, if the will of God be so, that ye suffer for well doing, than for evil doing"?

A: Peter (1 Peter 3:17)

DAY 229

Morning

Q: What cousin of Barnabas, who temporarily deserted the ministry, caused a falling out between Barnabas and the apostle Paul?

A: John Mark (Acts 15:37–40)

Evening

Q: Whose friends sat with him for seven days and nights without speaking?

A: Job's (Job 2:11–13)

DAY 230

Morning

Q: What did Peter do in defense of Jesus after His accusers arrived in the garden of Gethsemane?

A: Cut off the ear of the high priest's servant (John 18:10)

Evening

Q: What office did Judas occupy among the apostles?

A: Treasurer (John 13:29)

Morning

Q: What did the first angels mentioned in the Bible hold?

A: A flaming sword (Genesis 3:24)

Evening

Q: How did Mary Magdalene, Joanna, and Susanna assist with Jesus' ministry?

A: Financially; they "ministered unto him of their substance" (Luke 8:1-3)

Morning

Q: What woman had a dream about Jesus?

A: Pontius Pilate's wife (Matthew 27:19)

Evening

Q: Ahab, as king of Israel, ruled from what city?

A: Samaria (1 Kings 16:28-29)

Morning

Q: Where was David when he first spied Bathsheba?

A: On the roof of the king's house (2 Samuel 11:2–3)

Evening

Q: How many people were in Noah's ark?

A: Eight (Genesis 7:13)

Morning

Q: For what did the soldiers gamble near Jesus' cross?

A: His clothing (John 19:23–24)

Evening

Q: Which prophet was directed by the Lord to take a prostitute as a wife?

A: Hosea (Hosea 1:2)

Morning

Q: What did Gideon call the altar he built?

A: Jehovahshalom, or the Lord Is Peace
(Judges 6:24)

Evening

Q: Who said the law was our "schoolmaster to bring us into Christ"?

A: The apostle Paul (Galatians 1:1; 3:24)

Morning

Q: What did Moses throw into bitter water to make it sweet?

A: A tree (Exodus 15:24-25)

Evening

Q: In what land had Moses been living before he heard God's voice from a burning bush?

A: Midian (Exodus 3:1-4)

Morning

Q: Who once thought Jesus was a gardener?

A: Mary Magdalene (John 20:11, 15)

Evening

Q: How many husbands had the Samaritan woman at the well been married to?

A: Five (John 4:18)

Morning

Q: In the sentence, "The LORD shut him in," what door did God close?

A: The door of Noah's ark (Genesis 7:13-16)

Evening

Q: How many women did Jacob have children by?

A: Four—Rachel, Leah, Bilhah, and Zilpah (Genesis 35:23-26)

Morning

Q: In the parable of the prodigal son, what gifts did the father bestow upon his returning son?

A: A robe, a ring, and shoes (Luke 15:22)

Evening

Q: What is the last word in the Bible?

A: Amen (Revelation 22:21)

Morning

Q: After losing his hair, how did Samson regain his strength?

A: He prayed for it (Judges 16:28-29)

Evening

Q: Which Bible book records the phrase "the skin of my teeth"?

A: Job (Job 19:20)

DAY 241

Morning

Q: What did Peter promise those who humbled themselves "under the mighty hand of God"?

A: "He may exalt you in due time." (1 Peter 5:6)

Evening

Q: How many years did Noah live after the flood?

A: 350 (Genesis 9:28)

DAY 242

Morning

Q: What tribal background did King Saul and the apostle Paul have in common?

A: Benjamin (1 Samuel 9:1-2; Philippians 3:5)

Evening

Q: What did Jesus offer when He said, "Come unto me, all ye that labour and are heavy laden"?

A: Rest (Matthew 11:28)

Morning

Q: What were the chief priests and Pilate afraid that the disciples might try to do?

A: *Steal the body of Jesus (Matthew 27:62-66)*

Evening

Q: To whom did Paul address the words, "Not by works of righteousness which we have done, but according to his mercy he saved us"?

A: *Titus (Titus 3:5)*

Morning

Q: What two men were helped by ravens?

A: *Noah and Elijah (Genesis 8:6-7; 1 Kings 17:1-7)*

Evening

Q: What was Abel's occupation?

A: *Shepherd (Genesis 4:2)*

DAY 245

Morning

Q: What did Martha warn Jesus about when He went into the tomb of Lazarus?

A: The smell (John 11:39)

Evening

Q: Who cried when he heard a rooster crowing?

A: Peter (Matthew 26:75)

DAY 246

Morning

Q: What did Pharaoh do when the firstborn child in every Egyptian home died?

A: Let the Israelites leave his country (Exodus 12:29–33)

Evening

Q: According to the apostle Paul, to whom do "all things work together for good"?

A: "To them that love God" (Romans 8:28)

DAY 247

Morning

Q: After Jesus' resurrection, what did He tell the disciples to wait for before they left Jerusalem?

A: The Holy Spirit (Luke 24:49; Acts 1:7-8)

Evening

Q: Under Old Testament law what percentage of a man's wealth was he supposed to give to God?

A: 10 percent, a tithe (Leviticus 27:28-34)

DAY 248

Morning

Q: What disaster caused Jacob to send his sons from Canaan to Egypt?

A: Famine (Genesis 42:1-5)

Evening

Q: Who was betrayed for eleven hundred pieces of silver?

A: Samson (Judges 16:5)

DAY 249

Morning

Q: What happened to astonish Peter's believing companions as he preached to Cornelius?

A: *The Holy Spirit fell on the Gentiles (Acts 10:44-45)*

Evening

Q: Whom did God choose to do Moses' public speaking for him?

A: *Moses' brother, Aaron (Exodus 4:14-16)*

DAY 250

Morning

Q: How did Paul express the appeal to the lost on Christ's behalf?

A: *"Be ye reconciled to God" (2 Corinthians 5:20)*

Evening

Q: To what island did the apostle Paul assign Titus to work?

A: *Crete (Titus 1:5)*

DAY 251

Morning

Q: What transportation disaster befell the apostle Paul as he was traveling to Rome to stand trial before Caesar?

A: Shipwreck (Acts 27:21–44)

Evening

Q: Approximately how many men did Jesus feed with five loaves and two fishes?

A: Five thousand (Matthew 14:15–21)

DAY 252

Morning

Q: What did David use to actually kill Goliath?

A: A sword (1 Samuel 17:51)

Evening

Q: What sneaky predator did Jesus refer to in describing King Herod?

A: The fox (Luke 13:32)

DAY 253

Morning

Q: What is the only weapon that Jesus is said to have held?

A: A scourge, or whip (John 2:13-15)

Evening

Q: What king had three men thrown into a fiery furnace?

A: Nebuchadnezzar (Daniel 3:19-23)

DAY 254

Morning

Q: How can you be sure a prophecy is not from God?

A: It doesn't come true (Deuteronomy 18:21-22)

Evening

Q: What church did John describe as one with an "open door" because of its faithfulness?

A: Philadelphia (Revelation 3:7-8)

Morning

Q: Whom did Jesus intercede for while He was on the cross?

A: A repentant thief (Luke 23:39-43)

Evening

Q: In what mountains did Noah's ark come to rest?

A: The mountains of Ararat (Genesis 8:4)

Morning

Q: What does the Bible say oak, poplar, and elm trees have in common?

A: Good shade (Hosea 4:13)

Evening

Q: When God made woman, what was Adam doing?

A: Sleeping (Genesis 2:21-23)

Morning

Q: What sparkling substance does the writer of Proverbs compare to the poison of a viper?

A: Wine (Proverbs 23:31-32)

Evening

Q: What did David do in front of servant girls, making his wife angry?

A: Dance (2 Samuel 6:16-23)

Morning

Q: What did Daniel say he wouldn't do with the king of Babylon's meat and wine?

A: Defile himself (Daniel 1:8)

Evening

Q: What Israelite commander saw twenty-two thousand warriors—more than two-thirds of his army—desert when given the chance?

A: Gideon (Judges 7:1-3)

DAY 259

Morning

Q: On what basis did Christ say a person would be rewarded at His coming?

A: According to his works (Matthew 16:27)

Evening

Q: How many Bible books are known to be written by women?

A: None

DAY 260

Morning

Q: What musical instrument did Miriam, Aaron's sister, play?

A: A timbrel, or tambourine (Exodus 15:20)

Evening

Q: How many brothers did Jesus have?

A: Four: James, Joses, Juda, and Simon (Mark 6:3)

DAY 261

Morning

Q: What kind of chariot carried Elijah to heaven in a whirlwind?

A: A chariot of fire (2 Kings 2:11)

Evening

Q: How many days did Jonah spend in the belly of a "great fish"?

A: Three (Jonah 1:17)

DAY 262

Morning

Q: What did Jesus say is "fixed" between heaven and hell?

A: A "great gulf" or "great chasm" (Luke 16:19-31)

Evening

Q: Which book of the Bible mentions the constellations Pleiades and Orion?

A: Job (9:9, 38:31)

Morning

Q: Which book in the Bible does not mention the name *God*?

A: The book of Esther

Evening

Q: Who does the Bible describe as "very meek, above all the men which were upon the face of the earth"?

A: Moses (Numbers 12:3)

Morning

Q: Which two friends of Jesus prepared His body for burial?

A: Joseph of Arimathea and Nicodemus (John 19:38–41)

Evening

Q: According to the Beatitudes, who will inherit the earth?

A: The meek (Matthew 5:5)

DAY 265

Morning

Q: How was Moses' face different after he talked to God on Mount Sinai?

A: It shone (Exodus 34:29-35)

Evening

Q: On which of the six days of creation did God create birds?

A: Fifth (Genesis 1:20-23)

DAY 266

Morning

Q: After whose death did Jesus want to be alone?

A: John the Baptist's (Matthew 14:1-13)

Evening

Q: To whom did God say, "There shall no man see me, and live"?

A: Moses (Exodus 33:17-20)

DAY 267

Morning

Q: What animal tried to avoid an angel three times?

A: A donkey (Numbers 22:22-35)

Evening

Q: Which of Noah's sons saw him drunk and naked?

A: Ham (Genesis 9:20-22)

DAY 268

Morning

Q: What was Zacharias' family arguing about before he wrote down a single word?

A: What to name his new baby (Luke 1:59-63)

Evening

Q: According to Jesus, at what time of day does a red sky mean good weather for the next day?

A: Evening (Matthew 16:2)

Morning

Q: What did Moses do when he saw the Israelites' golden calf idol?

A: Broke the tablets with the Ten Commandments written on them (Exodus 31:18; 32:19)

Evening

Q: Which Old Testament book predicted hundreds of years in advance that Jesus' hands and feet would be pierced?

A: Psalms (Psalm 22:16)

Morning

Q: As Jesus ascended into heaven, who told the disciples He would return in like manner?

A: Two men dressed in white (Acts 1:9-11)

Evening

Q: Which of the ten plagues brought frogs on the land of Egypt?

A: Second (Exodus 8:1-4)

Morning

Q: What two brothers were described as being one "hairy," one "smooth"?

A: Esau and Jacob (Genesis 27:11)

Evening

Q: In how many Bible stories is Jesus described as writing?

A: Only one (John 8:1–11)

Morning

Q: What did Mary use to wipe perfume off Jesus' feet?

A: Her hair (John 12:3)

Evening

Q: What is the shortest verse in the King James Bible?

A: "Jesus wept" (John 11:35)

Morning

Q: What did King Darius do to Daniel because Daniel prayed to God?

A: Cast him into the lions' den (Daniel 6:11-27)

Evening

Q: Which prophet predicted that Jesus would be betrayed for thirty pieces of silver?

A: Zechariah (Zechariah 11:12-13)

Morning

Q: How was the birth of John the Baptist a miracle?

A: His mother was old (Luke 1:36)

Evening

Q: How many times did Noah send a dove out of the ark?

A: Three (Genesis 8:7-12)

DAY 275

Morning

Q: What site did Abraham purchase as a family burial place?

A: The cave of Machpelah (Genesis 23:19-20)

Evening

Q: Who placed a sign above Jesus on the cross, reading "JESUS OF NAZARETH THE KING OF THE JEWS"?

A: Pontius Pilate (John 19:19)

DAY 276

Morning

Q: Why did Jesus' relative John spend a lot of time at the Jordan River?

A: He baptized there (Matthew 3:1-6)

Evening

Q: To whom did Jesus quote the book of Deuteronomy three times?

A: Satan (Matthew 4:1-11)

DAY 277

Morning

Q: Who did the Israelites protect by putting lamb's blood on their doors?

A: Their firstborn children (Exodus 12:3-7, 12-13)

Evening

Q: Who succeeded Moses as leader of the Israelites?

A: Joshua (Joshua 1:1-10)

DAY 278

Morning

Q: As He was being crucified, whom did Jesus place in John's care?

A: Mary, his mother (John 19:26, 27)

Evening

Q: What kind of branches did crowds lay in front of Jesus as He rode into Jerusalem?

A: Palm (John 12:13)

DAY 279

Morning

Q: Why did God tell Abraham to sacrifice Isaac and later stop him?

A: To test his obedience (Genesis 22:1-18)

Evening

Q: Who offered more than five hundred animals to his brother as a peace gift?

A: Jacob (Genesis 32:13-18)

DAY 280

Morning

Q: What did the Pharisees once blame Jesus' disciples for doing on the Sabbath?

A: Picking corn, or grain (Matthew 12:1-8)

Evening

Q: How much older was Aaron than his brother Moses?

A: Three years (Exodus 7:7)

DAY 281

Morning

Q: What happened to the men who threw Shadrach, Meshach, and Abednego into the fiery furnace?

A: They were killed by the fire (Daniel 3:22–23)

Evening

Q: Whom did Mary visit for three months after talking to an angel?

A: Her relative Elisabeth (Luke 1:39–56)

DAY 282

Morning

Q: Who helped the disciples remember everything Jesus told them?

A: The Holy Ghost, or Spirit (John 14:26)

Evening

Q: How old was Abram when he obeyed God by moving from Haran to Canaan?

A: Seventy-five (Genesis 12:4)

DAY 283

Morning

Q: What apostle did Paul accuse of being a hypocrite?

A: Peter (Galatians 2:11-14)

Evening

Q: Who was famous for saying, "As for me and my house, we will serve the LORD?"

A: Joshua (Joshua 24:2, 15)

DAY 284

Morning

Q: What happened to Jesus while He was in the desert for forty days and nights?

A: He was tempted by Satan (Matthew 4:1-2)

Evening

Q: What did the prophet Daniel predict that King Nebuchadnezzar would eat?

A: Grass (Daniel 4:18, 25)

DAY 285

Morning

Q: What sign reminds us that God will never again flood the whole earth?

A: The rainbow (Genesis 9:11-13)

Evening

Q: To whom was Jesus speaking when He said His followers should forgive "seventy times seven" times?

A: Peter (Matthew 18:21-22)

DAY 286

Morning

Q: What famous words are found in both Luke 11 and Matthew 6?

A: The Lord's Prayer (Luke 11:2-4; Matthew 6:9-13)

Evening

Q: What boy, destined to become king at age eight, had his birth foretold by a man of God to the wicked King Jeroboam?

A: Josiah (1 Kings 13:1-3)

Morning

Q: What animal did Samson kill with his bare hands?

A: A lion (Judges 14:5-6)

Evening

Q: Why did Jesus say His followers should "be of good cheer"?

A: Because "I have overcome the world" (John 16:33)

Morning

Q: What important event happened at "the place of a skull"?

A: Jesus was crucified (John 19:16-18)

Evening

Q: What follower of Jesus was martyred by an angry, screaming crowd, after a critical speech to the Sanhedrin?

A: Stephen (Acts 7:51-60)

DAY 289

Morning

Q: What did Jacob trade for Esau's birthright?

A: Bread and lentil pottage, or stew
(Genesis 25:32–34)

Evening

Q: What long-dead prophet's bones brought another dead man back to life?

A: Elisha (2 Kings 13:21)

DAY 290

Morning

Q: What did Pilate say to the crowd when he questioned Jesus the second time and washed his hands?

A: "I am innocent of the blood of this just person"
(Matthew 27:13–14, 24)

Evening

Q: Who killed two people with one spear?

A: Phinehas (Numbers 25:7–8)

DAY 291

Morning

Q: What young king removed all the mediums and spiritists from Judah, as required in the book of the law found by his priest, Hilkiah?

A: Josiah (2 Kings 22:1–8; 23:24–25)

Evening

Q: Who commanded, "Whatsoever ye do in word or deed, do all in the name of the Lord Jesus"?

A: The apostle Paul (Colossians 3:17)

DAY 292

Morning

Q: What did James say about the one who "knoweth to do good, and doeth it not"?

A: "To him it is sin" (James 4:17)

Evening

Q: How many Bible books did John the Baptist write?

A: None

Morning

Q: What do the wives of Noah, Lot, and Job have in common?

A: None are mentioned by name

Evening

Q: What Bible character had his name changed to Zaphnath-paaneah?

A: Joseph (Genesis 41:45)

Morning

Q: What two Old Testament men did Jesus talk to during the Transfiguration?

A: Moses and Elias, or Elijah (Matthew 17:1-3)

Evening

Q: In what town did Jesus perform His first miracle?

A: Cana of Galilee (John 2:1-11)

DAY 295

Morning

Q: What was the reason for the first wind recorded in the Bible?

A: To clear the floodwaters from the earth (Genesis 8:1)

Evening

Q: Which Bible book has the most chapters?

A: Psalms—150 of them!

DAY 296

Morning

Q: What did an angel often come down to Bethesda to stir up?

A: The waters of its pool (John 5:2–4)

Evening

Q: What are the colors of the four horses that are mentioned in Revelation 6?

A: White, red, black, and pale (Revelation 6)

Morning

Q: How did Absalom get caught in a tree?

A: By his hair (2 Samuel 18:9)

Evening

Q: What man fell down laughing when God said his old wife would have a baby?

A: Abraham (Genesis 17:17)

Morning

Q: What kind of man did Jesus say builds his house upon the sand?

A: A foolish one (Matthew 7:26)

Evening

Q: What did Jesus say a person must have in order to see miracles?

A: Faith (Matthew 21:21)

DAY 299

Morning

Q: What did God stop from being built by confusing man's language?

A: The tower of Babel (Genesis 11:1-9)

Evening

Q: What ruler tried to kill the prophet Elijah?

A: Queen Jezebel (1 Kings 19:1-2)

DAY 300

Morning

Q: What was the name of Aaron's wife?

A: Elisheba (Exodus 6:23)

Evening

Q: How many years had one poor man waited at the pool of Bethesda to be healed?

A: Thirty-eight (John 5:2-5)

Morning

Q: Which three men in the Bible were said to have each killed a lion?

A: Samson, David, and Benaiah (Judges 14:5-6; 1 Samuel 17:34-35; 2 Samuel 23:20)

Evening

Q: How many tablets in total did Moses bring down from Mount Sinai?

A: Four (Exodus 32:15, 19; 34:29)

Morning

Q: How did the Jews react to the newly converted Saul's bold witness for Christ?

A: They tried to kill him (Acts 9:22-23)

Evening

Q: What did the Israelites call the brass serpent Moses had made to save them from a plague, but which they later burned incense to?

A: Nehushtan (2 Kings 18:4)

DAY 303

Morning

Q: Into what river did Pharaoh cast Israelite baby boys?

A: Not named in the King James Version, but identified as the Nile in modern translations (Exodus 1:22)

Evening

Q: Who made the first human clothing out of animal skins?

A: God (Genesis 3:21)

DAY 304

Morning

Q: How did the friends of a paralyzed man get him through the crowds to be healed by Jesus?

A: They lowered him through a roof (Mark 2:3–12)

Evening

Q: What part of the altar was to be grasped by someone seeking sanctuary?

A: The horns (1 Kings 2:28)

DAY 305

Morning

Q: To what beloved hill, which "abideth forever,"
are those who trust in the Lord compared to?

A: Mount Zion (Psalm 125:1)

Evening

Q: What did the Philistines return with the ark of
the covenant when they returned it to Israel?

A: Five gold mice and five gold emerods,
or tumors (1 Samuel 6:4, 11)

DAY 306

Morning

Q: To what place did Peter and John race?

A: Jesus' tomb (John 20:1–4)

Evening

Q: What letter of the alphabet begins the names of
the most books of the Bible?

A: J (Joshua, Judges, Job, Jeremiah, Joel, Jonah,
John, James, 1 John, 2 John, 3 John, Jude)

DAY 307

Morning

Q: What was three hundred cubits by fifty cubits by thirty cubits in size?

A: Noah's ark (Genesis 6:13-15)

Evening

Q: What temptress of the Old Testament lived in the Valley of Sorek?

A: Delilah (Judges 16:4)

DAY 308

Morning

Q: What, according to Corinthians, is the goal of the Christian athlete's training?

A: An incorruptible crown (1 Corinthians 9:25)

Evening

Q: How many days did the spies sent by Moses search out the promised land?

A: Forty (Numbers 13:25)

DAY 309

Morning

Q: What special gift did God give Daniel?

A: The ability to understand visions and dreams (Daniel 1:17)

Evening

Q: What type of bird did Jesus say would not fall to the ground without God knowing?

A: A sparrow (Matthew 10:29)

DAY 310

Morning

Q: In the parable of the prodigal son, what job did the desperate young man take?

A: Feeding swine (Luke 15:15)

Evening

Q: When did Jesus tell Peter, "Blessed art thou, Simon Barjona"?

A: After Peter said, "Thou art the Christ" (Matthew 16:16-17)

DAY 311

Morning

Q: In what part of their houses were the ancient Israelites to write God's commands, as a daily reminder to themselves and their children?

A: Doorposts (Deuteronomy 11:18-20)

Evening

Q: Which of the seven churches of Revelation did Jesus say was blind?

A: Laodicea (Revelation 3:14, 17)

DAY 312

Morning

Q: Which two disciples were sons of Zebedee?

A: James and John (Matthew 4:21)

Evening

Q: How many brothers did Abram have?

A: Two—Nahor and Haran (Genesis 11:27)

Morning

Q: How many wives did Israel's King Solomon have?

A: Seven hundred (1 Kings 11:1–3)

Evening

Q: What child, when he was called by God in the night, said, "Speak; for thy servant heareth"?

A: Samuel (1 Samuel 3:10)

Morning

Q: What part of the body does the Bible say can be evil and full of deadly poison?

A: The tongue (James 3:8)

Evening

Q: Who was Israel's king when Assyria took the nation captive?

A: Hoshea (2 Kings 17:6)

DAY 315

Morning

Q: What quality in a man, according to the Proverbs, makes him "better than the mighty"?

A: Being "slow to anger," or patient (Proverbs 16:32)

Evening

Q: In what church were Jesus' followers first called Christians?

A: Antioch (Acts 11:26)

DAY 316

Morning

Q: What two men in the Bible walked on water?

A: Jesus and Peter (Matthew 14:26-31)

Evening

Q: Who were the Old Testament cities of refuge set up to protect?

A: People who killed someone accidentally (Numbers 35:15)

DAY 317

Morning

Q: What was Jesus' first miracle?

A: He turned water into wine at a wedding feast (John 2:1–11)

Evening

Q: What woman helped her son trick his father into giving him a blessing?

A: Rebekah (Genesis 27:1–17)

DAY 318

Morning

Q: Who really took Jesus' life?

A: No one—He chose to die for us (John 10:18)

Evening

Q: Who made a covenant with his eyes never to look on a young woman?

A: Job (Job 31:1)

Morning

Q: What did Samson lie about three times?

A: The secret of his strength (Judges 16:5–15)

Evening

Q: How many times a day did Daniel kneel and pray?

A: Three (Daniel 6:10)

Morning

Q: How did Judas identify Jesus in the garden of Gethsemane?

A: With a kiss (Mark 14:32, 44–45)

Evening

Q: How many days did the waters stay upon the earth after the great flood?

A: 150 (Genesis 7:24)

DAY 321

Morning

Q: Where was Joseph when the king, wanting the interpretation of a dream, called for him?

A: In a dungeon (Genesis 41:14)

Evening

Q: What evangelist had four daughters who prophesied?

A: Philip (Acts 21:8-9)

DAY 322

Morning

Q: What did Jesus say was the "first and great commandment"?

A: "Love the Lord thy God" (Matthew 22:37-38)

Evening

Q: About whom did Jesus say, "I have not found so great faith, no, not in Israel"?

A: A centurion (Matthew 8:8-10)

DAY 323

Morning

Q: What construction project did Nehemiah bring to a successful conclusion despite the mocking and threats of enemies?

A: Rebuilding the wall of Jerusalem
(Nehemiah 4:4-5; 6:15)

Evening

Q: How many gems were on the high priest's breastplate?

A: Twelve (Exodus 28:21)

DAY 324

Morning

Q: What special tree is made available to those whose names are "written in the Lamb's book of life"?

A: The tree of life (Revelation 21:27; 22:14)

Evening

Q: Out of what city was the apostle Paul lowered in a basket over the wall?

A: Damascus (Acts 9:19-25)

DAY 325

Morning

Q: After Samson was captured and blinded, what job did the Philistines give him at Gaza?

A: Grinding at the prison mill (Judges 16:20–21)

Evening

Q: Who did Abraham marry after Sarah died?

A: Keturah (Genesis 25:1)

DAY 326

Morning

Q: What did Mary, the mother of Jesus, do after He ascended into heaven?

A: She went to an upstairs room with many others (Acts 1:10–14)

Evening

Q: Which spiritual gift did Paul say the church at Corinth was misusing?

A: Speaking in tongues (1 Corinthians 14:1–4)

Morning

Q: When the children of Israel left slavery in Egypt, what happened to the bones of Joseph?

A: Moses took the bones with him (Exodus 13:18-19)

Evening

Q: According to the Psalms, what declares the glory of God?

A: The heavens (Psalm 19:1)

Morning

Q: What did Jesus invite "doubting Thomas" to do that would affirm His resurrection?

A: Place his hands in the nail prints (John 20:26-27)

Evening

Q: How many years did Noah spend preparing the ark as God told him?

A: One hundred (Genesis 5:32; 7:11)

DAY 329

Morning

Q: Why did Hannah choose the name *Samuel* for her son?

A: It means "asked of the Lord"—she had prayed for a son (1 Samuel 1:20)

Evening

Q: Who explained the writing on Belshazzar's wall?

A: Daniel (Daniel 5:17-31)

DAY 330

Morning

Q: What did Jesus endure "for the joy that was set before him"?

A: The cross (Hebrews 12:2)

Evening

Q: What two women are named in the "Faith Hall of Fame" in Hebrews 11?

A: Sarah and Rahab (verses 11, 31)

DAY 331

Morning

Q: Why did Joseph's brothers dip his coat in blood?

A: To make their father think he was dead (Genesis 37:29-33)

Evening

Q: What did God, through His prophet Samuel, say is "better than sacrifice"?

A: Obedience (1 Samuel 15:22)

DAY 332

Morning

Q: What did Agabus prophesy when Paul was in Antioch?

A: A severe famine (Acts 11:25-28)

Evening

Q: How did John the Baptist die?

A: He was beheaded by King Herod (John 14:6-10)

DAY 333

Morning

Q: Why was Hezekiah like no king of Judah either before or after him?

A: He followed the Lord and kept the commands given to Moses (2 Kings 18:5-6)

Evening

Q: How is the Word of God described in the Ephesians 6 "armour of God" passage?

A: "The sword of the Spirit" (Ephesians 6:17)

DAY 334

Morning

Q: What response did the woman of Canaan give when Jesus said He was sent to the lost sheep of Israel?

A: "Yet the dogs eat of the crumbs which fall from their masters' table" (Matthew 15:22-27)

Evening

Q: What book of the Bible contains the words, "A time to plant, and a time to pluck up that which is planted"?

A: Ecclesiastes (Ecclesiastes 3:2)

Morning

Q: With whom did David make a covenant to protect each other?

A: Saul's son Jonathan (1 Samuel 20:1-23)

Evening

Q: What was Esther's Hebrew name?

A: Hadassah (Esther 2:7)

Morning

Q: What did Jesus do with His hands just prior to His ascension?

A: Lifted them up and blessed the disciples (Luke 24:50-51)

Evening

Q: What kind of tree did the judge Deborah sit under?

A: Palm (Judges 4:4-5)

Morning

Q: What specific date does the Bible say was the first day of the flood?

A: The seventeenth day of the second month (Genesis 7:11)

Evening

Q: Before He began preaching, what was Jesus' trade?

A: Carpentry (Mark 6:3)

Morning

Q: According to the apostle Paul, how many people saw the risen Jesus at one time?

A: About five hundred (1 Corinthians 15:6)

Evening

Q: Who had his name changed to Belteshazzar?

A: Daniel (Daniel 1:7)

Morning

Q: What was the first question that Philip asked the Ethiopian eunuch reading in his chariot?

A: "Understandest thou what thou readest?" (Acts 8:30)

Evening

Q: What Jewish feast was associated with bitter herbs?

A: Unleavened Bread, or Passover (Exodus 12)

Morning

Q: Why did Naomi ask the people of Bethlehem to call her "Mara"?

A: It means "bitter," and she said, "The Almighty hath dealt very bitterly with me" (Ruth 1:19-20)

Evening

Q: What angel told Zacharias that his old wife would have a baby?

A: Gabriel (Luke 1:18-19)

DAY 341

Morning

Q: Who said, "What have I done unto thee, that thou hast smitten me these three times?"

A: Balaam's donkey (Numbers 22:28)

Evening

Q: What empire's laws, once made, could not be changed?

A: The Medes and the Persians (Daniel 6:8)

DAY 342

Morning

Q: Who did John the Baptist call a "generation of vipers"?

A. The Pharisees and Sadducees (Matthew 3:1, 7)

Evening

Q: Who was killed so King Ahab of Israel could take his vineyard?

A: Naboth (1 Kings 21:1-16)

Morning

Q: When Job was tested, how many sons and daughters did he have?

A: Ten—seven sons and three daughters (Job 1:1-2)

Evening

Q: Who was Bathsheba's first husband?

A: Uriah (2 Samuel 11:3)

Morning

Q: What can "they that are in the flesh" not do?

A: Please God (Romans 8:8)

Evening

Q: When do the Proverbs say a thief is not despised?

A: When he steals food because he is starving (Proverbs 6:30)

DAY 345

Morning

Q: In return for her help in hiding them, what did the Israelite spies promise Rahab?

A: *To spare her family when Jericho was attacked (Joshua 2:1, 12-14)*

Evening

Q: How long did it take Solomon to build God's temple?

A: *Seven years (1 Kings 6:37-38)*

DAY 346

Morning

Q: What does the apostle Paul call the "first commandment with promise"?

A: *"Honour thy father and mother" (Ephesians 6:2)*

Evening

Q: What husband and wife, coworkers with Paul, taught Apollos the way of God more accurately?

A: *Aquila and Priscilla (Acts 18:26)*

DAY 347

Morning

Q: What patriarch used a stone for a pillow?

A: *Jacob (Genesis 28:10-11)*

Evening

Q: What is the falling star of Revelation 8 called?

A: *Wormwood (Revelation 8:10-11)*

DAY 348

Morning

Q: What three-word phrase did the resurrected Jesus repeat while reinstating Peter?

A: *"Feed my sheep [or lambs]" (John 21:15-19)*

Evening

Q: What silversmith of Ephesus, who made shrines for the goddess Diana, started a riot to get rid of Paul?

A: *Demetrius (Acts 19:24)*

Morning

Q: After Moses became angry with the Israelites for disobeying God, what did he do?

A: He interceded for them with God
(Exodus 32:30-32)

Evening

Q: To whom was Jesus speaking when He said, "He that hath seen me hath seen the Father"?

A: Philip (John 14:8-9)

Morning

Q: Who did King Herod send out to find Jesus?

A: The wise men (Matthew 2:7-0)

Evening

Q: How did Pontius Pilate's wife describe Jesus?

A: "That just [or innocent] man" (Matthew 27:19)

DAY 351

Morning

Q: Why was Samuel chosen to be a judge over Eli's sons?

A: Because Eli's sons were evil (1 Samuel 2:12; 3:20)

Evening

Q: How did Jesus reply when His critics said that He was under fifty years old and could not have seen Abraham?

A: "Before Abraham was, I am" (John 8:58)

DAY 352

Morning

Q: What group of believers did Paul say would be the first resurrected?

A: "The dead in Christ" (1 Thessalonians 4:16)

Evening

Q: How many smooth stones did David have available for his fight with Goliath?

A: Five–though he only used one (1 Samuel 17:40)

DAY 353

Morning

Q: How old was Noah when the flood started?

A: Six hundred (Genesis 7:11)

Evening

Q: How did Judas Iscariot kill himself after betraying Jesus?

A: By hanging (Matthew 27:5)

DAY 354

Morning

Q: What type of people, according to the book of James, does God give grace to?

A: The humble (James 4:6)

Evening

Q: How was Nehemiah employed by the Persian king Artaxerxes?

A: He was cupbearer (Nehemiah 1:11)

Morning

Q: Which two kings are described as extremely tall?

A: Og and Saul (Deuteronomy 3:11; 1 Samuel 10:20-23)

Evening

Q: In speaking of Jesus, what did John the Baptist say he was unworthy to do?

A: Untie His shoes (Mark 1:7)

Morning

Q: When did the apostle Paul say Christians should set aside money for the Lord's offering?

A: "Upon the first day of the week" (1 Corinthians 16:1-2)

Evening

Q: How long was Zimri's reign, the shortest of the kings of Israel?

A: Seven days (1 Kings 16:15)

DAY 357

Morning

Q: Who did Job say were his brothers and "companions"?

A: Dragons [or jackals] and owls (Job 30:29)

Evening

Q: How many concubines—a kind of secondary wife—did King Solomon keep?

A: Three hundred (1 Kings 11:3)

DAY 358

Morning

Q: Where did the ascension of Jesus take place?

A: Near Bethany (Luke 24:50–51)

Evening

Q: Besides being priest of the most high God, what was Melchizedek king of?

A: Salem (Genesis 14:18)

Morning

Q: Why do the proverbs advise us, "Boast not thyself of to morrow"?

A: We don't know what a day will bring (Proverbs 27:1)

Evening

Q: What otherwise good king was struck with leprosy for burning incense in the temple?

A: Uzziah (2 Chronicles 26:19)

Morning

Q: What two destroyers, according to Jesus, will never "corrupt" one's treasures in heaven?

A: Moth and rust (Matthew 6:20)

Evening

Q: What colors did Isaiah use to describe sin?

A: Crimson, red like scarlet (Isaiah 1:18)

DAY 361

Morning

Q: What family occurrences prompted Naomi to return to Bethlehem from Moab?

A: *The death of her husband and sons (Ruth 1:3–7, 19)*

Evening

Q: What group of people drowned in the Red Sea?

A: *Pharaoh's army (Exodus 14:28)*

DAY 362

Morning

Q: What did Philip say to overcome Nathaniel's disbelief that Jesus was the Messiah?

A: *"Come and see." (John 1:46)*

Evening

Q: What happened to the manna if the Israelites left it overnight?

A: *It spoiled and bred worms (Exodus 16:20)*

DAY 363

Morning

Q: Including the apostle Paul, how many people survived the wreck of his ship off Malta?

A: 276 (Acts 27:21-44)

Evening

Q: Who called the Lord "Thou God seest me"?

A: Hagar (Genesis 16:8, 13)

DAY 364

Morning

Q: How did Samson kill the Philistine rulers and a large number of celebrants honoring their god Dagon?

A: He knocked down two middle pillars of the building (Judges 16:27-30)

Evening

Q: Who is identified in scripture as "the archangel"?

A: Michael (Jude 9)

Morning

Q: What commendation did Enoch receive before he was taken from this life?

A: He pleased God (Hebrews 11:5)

Evening

Q: According to Paul, what is the supreme gift of the Spirit to believers?

A: Charity, or love (1 Corinthians 12:31; 13:13)

WANT *MORE* BIBLE TRIVIA?

So you think you know the Bible?
Prove it! The Bible's a big, serious book—
but it's also full of fun and fascinating
details lending itself to trivia quizzes. So
here's a collection of 1,000 questions, divided
into 100 categories, designed to see just
what you remember from God's Word.

Paperback / 978-1-64352-652-2